JACK THE RIPPER

New Clues to an Old Mystery

CHARLES B.LEO

Table of Contents

Chapter 1: The Foggy Streets of Whitechapel

Whitechapel in the late 19th century was one of the most notorious districts in London. Located in the East End, it was a densely populated area known for poverty, overcrowding, and crime. The streets were narrow and winding, with rows of tenement buildings that were often in poor condition. Many families lived in single rooms, and sanitation was a constant problem. Garbage piled up in the streets, and the Thames River nearby carried waste and sewage, giving the area a persistent foul smell. Fog, a common feature of London at the time, mixed with smoke from chimneys to create a thick, almost permanent haze that made it difficult to see clearly at night.

Life in Whitechapel was hard for most people. The majority of residents were working-class or poor, often surviving on very low wages. Many men worked as laborers, dock workers, or in small factories, while women took on domestic work, laundry, or prostitution. The latter was common because economic opportunities for women were limited. Streets like Dorset Street, Flower and Dean Street, and Buck's Row were infamous for prostitution, alcoholism, and petty crime. Crime rates were high, but serious violence, especially against women, started to gain wider attention during the Jack the Ripper murders.

The housing conditions in Whitechapel were overcrowded and unsanitary. Many families shared single rooms with little ventilation or proper plumbing. Diseases like tuberculosis, cholera, and typhus were common, and infant mortality rates were high. Public health services were limited, and medical care was often inaccessible to the poor. These harsh conditions created a backdrop of suffering and desperation, which the Ripper's crimes would later exploit.

The streets of Whitechapel were also poorly lit. Gas lamps were installed, but they were often spaced far apart, leaving many areas in near darkness at night. Alleyways and courtyards offered hiding spots for criminals, and residents were often wary of walking alone after dark. The area was filled with pubs, coffee houses, and small shops, but despite the commercial activity, life remained difficult for most people. Street markets offered cheap food, but they were crowded and unhygienic. People from all walks of life—sailors, laborers, beggars, and immigrants—mingled in the streets, creating a chaotic urban environment.

Whitechapel was also home to many immigrants, especially Jewish people fleeing persecution in Eastern Europe. By the 1880s, a large number of Jewish families had settled in the area, creating a community with its own businesses, schools, and religious institutions. However, tensions between local residents and immigrants sometimes led to discrimination and hostility. These social dynamics added complexity to the neighborhood, with different cultural and economic groups living side by side in close quarters.

The police presence in Whitechapel was noticeable but limited in effectiveness. The Metropolitan Police had stations nearby, but the large population and chaotic streets made law enforcement challenging. Officers often patrolled the streets on foot, but they struggled to prevent petty crime, much less the more serious acts that would later shock London. Many residents distrusted the police, believing they were either indifferent or corrupt. This distrust made it difficult for authorities to gather reliable information from witnesses or prevent crime.

Public transportation in the area was limited. Horse-drawn buses and cabs were available, but many people relied on walking. The close quarters of Whitechapel meant that noise and activity spilled into the streets, creating a sense of constant movement. Markets opened early in the morning, and the smell of cooked food mixed with refuse and smoke. Children played in alleys, and vendors shouted to sell their goods, all under the watch of anxious residents trying to survive.

Whitechapel's reputation for crime and danger was well known throughout London. Newspapers often reported on assaults, thefts, and murders, painting a picture of a neighborhood where violence was routine. The press also exaggerated certain stories, adding to the sense of fear and fascination surrounding the district. For outsiders, Whitechapel represented the darker side of Victorian London, a place where poverty, crime, and human suffering intersected.

The geography of Whitechapel itself added to the danger. Narrow lanes, dead-end alleys, and hidden courtyards made it easy for criminals to escape unnoticed. Buildings were tall and closely packed, limiting visibility from the street. Residents had to be cautious at all hours, especially women, who were vulnerable to attack while walking alone. At night, the fog and darkness combined to create a sense of unease, making it easy for crimes to occur without witnesses.

In addition to the physical dangers, social issues made Whitechapel a difficult place to live. Alcoholism was widespread, particularly among men, and many people relied on cheap gin to numb hunger or escape daily struggles. Gangs and street violence were common, and disputes could turn deadly. Families struggled to make ends meet, often going without adequate food or heating. Children frequently had to work or beg to contribute to the household, and education was minimal.

Despite the challenges, Whitechapel was a vibrant community. People supported one another through informal networks, sharing resources and helping neighbors in times of need. Markets, churches, and social clubs provided opportunities for connection and relief from daily hardships. However, the combination of poverty, crime, and social tension made it an environment where fear and danger were ever-present.

The stage for Jack the Ripper's crimes was thus set. The foggy, dimly lit streets, the crowded and unsanitary housing, and the social struggles of Whitechapel created conditions that allowed a killer to operate with terrifying effectiveness. Residents lived in constant vigilance, aware that danger could strike at any moment. This chapter of London's history captures not only the physical and social environment of Whitechapel but also the mood of uncertainty, fear, and intrigue that defined the district during the time of the murders.

The mixture of fog, poverty, and crime meant that the streets of Whitechapel were both a home and a threat to those who lived there. It was a place where human suffering was visible, and danger lurked in the shadows. These conditions are essential to understanding how Jack the Ripper could commit his crimes and why the district became so infamous in the public imagination.

Chapter 2: The First Killings

The terror in Whitechapel began in the late summer of 1888, when the first of a series of brutal murders shocked London. These killings were unlike ordinary crimes; they were violent, targeted, and left a lasting impression on the public. The first widely recognized victim of Jack the Ripper was Mary Ann Nichols, whose death marked the start of a series that would come to define the East End of London for years.

Mary Ann Nichols was discovered on August 31, 1888, in Buck's Row, now called Durward Street. She was found early in the morning, lying face down in the street, her throat cut and her abdomen mutilated. Nichols was 43 years old and had lived a difficult life. She had struggled with poverty, unemployment, and alcoholism, and like many women in Whitechapel, she turned to prostitution to survive. Her death highlighted both the vulnerability of women in the area and the dangers of the dark, foggy streets at night.

The public reaction to Nichols' murder was immediate. Newspapers sensationalized the story, using dramatic language to capture readers' attention. The details of her death were horrifying, and the press emphasized the brutality and mystery surrounding the crime. Police were under pressure to solve the case quickly, but the conditions in Whitechapel made investigations challenging. Witnesses were scarce, streets were dark and crowded, and the sheer density of the population complicated efforts to gather information.

Only a few weeks later, the second recognized victim, Annie Chapman, was discovered. Chapman's body was found on September 8, 1888, in the backyard of 29 Hanbury Street. Like Nichols, her throat had been cut, and her abdomen mutilated. Chapman was in her late 40s and faced similar hardships, including poverty, homelessness, and reliance on prostitution to survive. Her death reinforced the idea that a single killer was operating in Whitechapel, targeting women who were vulnerable due to their social and economic circumstances.

Police officers and detectives began to notice patterns. The victims were all women living in poverty, and their bodies were found in secluded areas, often early in the morning. The killer appeared to have knowledge of anatomy, as the mutilations were precise. These observations suggested that the crimes were not random but calculated, and they caused fear not only in Whitechapel but throughout London. People became wary of walking alone at night, and women in particular faced heightened anxiety about their safety.

The third victim, Elizabeth Stride, was found on September 30, 1888, in Dutfield's Yard off Berner Street. Unlike the previous victims, Stride's body showed only a throat wound, with no further mutilation. This led some to speculate that the killer was interrupted or had been forced to flee before completing his attack. Stride was 44 years old and, like the others, struggled with poverty and made a living as a prostitute. Her death deepened the mystery, as it suggested a possible pattern but also raised questions about the killer's methods and intentions.

Later that same night, the fourth victim, Catherine Eddowes, was discovered in Mitre Square. Her murder was more violent than Stride's, with mutilations similar to those inflicted on Nichols and Chapman. Eddowes was 46 years old, a local woman who had also faced economic hardship and had lived a difficult life. Her body was discovered in a public square, increasing public fear because the attack had occurred in a relatively open space, showing the killer's boldness. The proximity of Stride and Eddowes' murders led police to suspect that the same person committed both, establishing the idea of a single serial killer.

The killings caused panic in Whitechapel. Women became afraid to go out at night, and even daytimes were tense due to rumors and warnings circulating in the community. The press played a significant role in spreading fear, with graphic descriptions of the crimes and speculation about the killer's identity. Public meetings were held, and community leaders urged vigilance, but the sense of helplessness persisted. Residents knew that law enforcement faced enormous challenges in such a chaotic environment.

Detectives worked tirelessly, following leads and interviewing witnesses, but clues were scarce. Many victims were known to associate with men who were part of the local underworld, making it difficult to separate credible leads from gossip. Some suspects were questioned, but few had strong connections to the murders. The complexity of Whitechapel's streets, combined with the limited forensic techniques of the time, made solving the crimes extremely difficult.

The series of killings also revealed social issues in Victorian London. Women like Nichols, Chapman, Stride, and Eddowes were marginalized due to poverty and their professions. Their vulnerability highlighted how economic hardship and social inequality could leave people exposed to violence. The murders drew attention not only to a criminal but also to broader problems, such as the lack of social support, inadequate housing, and limited opportunities for women.

By the end of 1888, Whitechapel was gripped by fear. The killer's identity remained unknown, and the pattern of targeting women living in vulnerable circumstances became clear. The first killings marked the beginning of a sequence that would captivate the public imagination, challenge police methods, and leave a lasting impact on the East End of London. These murders were not isolated incidents but the opening chapter of a terrifying and complex series of crimes that would remain unsolved and mysterious for generations.

Chapter 3: The Victims' Lives

The women who fell victim to Jack the Ripper were more than names in a newspaper; they were human beings with stories, struggles, and connections to their communities. Understanding their lives provides insight into the harsh realities of Whitechapel in the late 19th century and explains why these women were vulnerable to such violent crimes.

Mary Ann Nichols, the first widely recognized victim, was born in 1845 in London. She had experienced a life filled with hardship, including early widowhood and struggles with poverty. She moved frequently, taking on domestic work when possible, but economic pressures often forced her into prostitution. Nichols had children, but they were placed with relatives due to her unstable circumstances. Her day-to-day life involved navigating the difficult streets of Whitechapel, seeking work, shelter, and basic necessities. The instability and danger she faced every day were representative of many women in the area.

Annie Chapman, the second known victim, was born in 1841 and had lived through her own hardships. Widowed at a young age, she also turned to prostitution to survive. Chapman had four children, but like Nichols, her family life was disrupted by poverty and personal tragedy. She struggled with alcoholism, a common coping mechanism for women in Whitechapel who faced daily stress, abuse, and deprivation. Chapman's existence was precarious, reliant on temporary work and the kindness of others for food and shelter. Her vulnerability was heightened by the physical and social dangers of the East End.

Elizabeth Stride, discovered on September 30, 1888, came from Sweden. She moved to London in search of a better life but found herself living in poverty. Stride worked as a prostitute to survive and struggled with personal difficulties, including unstable housing and limited family support. She was known as a quiet and reserved woman, often trying to avoid trouble, yet her circumstances left her exposed to danger. Stride's murder was unusual in that her body showed only a throat wound, suggesting either an interrupted attack or a different motive, but it did not lessen the tragedy of her life cut short.

Catherine Eddowes, found the same night as Stride, had also faced significant challenges. Born in 1842, she had a difficult early life and suffered from alcoholism and poverty. Eddowes lived in several workhouses and shelters over her lifetime, struggling to find stable employment. She relied on prostitution as a means of survival, a common path for women with limited options. Eddowes' life illustrates the cyclical nature of poverty in Whitechapel, where limited opportunities, social stigma, and personal struggles created conditions of extreme vulnerability.

Other women, sometimes referred to as "Ripper victims" in broader discussions, shared similar circumstances. Many had been abandoned, widowed, or estranged from family. Economic hardship was a constant factor, forcing women to work in dangerous or stigmatized professions. They often faced violence, both domestic and from strangers, and lived in overcrowded, unsanitary conditions. Their lives were marked by instability, uncertainty, and the need to navigate a society that offered them little protection.

The social conditions of Whitechapel amplified these vulnerabilities. Women had few employment opportunities, and the wages for domestic work or factory labor were often insufficient to survive. Many resorted to prostitution, not out of desire but necessity, exposing them to criminal elements and violent attacks. Alcoholism, poor nutrition, and inadequate healthcare further weakened their physical and mental resilience, making them easy targets for a predator like Jack the Ripper.

Community networks existed, however, to support women in distress. Charitable organizations, workhouses, and shelters provided food, temporary lodging, and minimal medical care. Religious institutions often offered guidance and assistance.

Yet these supports were limited, and the needs of the population far outstripped the available resources. Women like Nichols, Chapman, Stride, and Eddowes had to navigate this precarious environment daily, relying on informal connections or small acts of generosity to survive.

Understanding the victims' lives also involves recognizing their humanity beyond poverty and crime. They had personalities, relationships, and dreams, even if these were constrained by their circumstances. Friends and neighbors remembered them as people who laughed, worried, and cared for others. By looking closely at their lives, historians and writers can reconstruct the social fabric of Whitechapel and gain a clearer picture of why these women were in the wrong place at the wrong time.

The murders highlighted not only the brutality of the killer but also the fragility of women's lives in Victorian London. Their deaths exposed gaps in public safety, social services, and policing. Whitechapel's women faced threats daily, and the Ripper's actions amplified existing fears. The public fascination with the case was partly due to the vulnerability of these women and the social commentary their lives represented.

These lives, marked by hardship and resilience, are central to understanding the Ripper story. Each woman had her struggles, and their experiences reflected broader issues in East London society: poverty, limited opportunity, and social marginalization. They were ordinary people living in extraordinary circumstances, and their murders revealed the dark realities of life in the foggy streets of Whitechapel.

By examining their biographies and daily challenges, one gains a deeper comprehension of the environment in which Jack the Ripper operated. It also underscores that the victims were not merely statistics or sensational headlines— they were human beings whose stories matter in their own right. Their lives, though brief and often tragic, offer insight into the social, economic, and cultural conditions that shaped Whitechapel at the time of the murders.

Chapter 4: The Investigation Begins

The investigation into the Jack the Ripper murders began immediately after the first killings, but it faced extraordinary challenges. Whitechapel in 1888 was a crowded, chaotic district, and the Metropolitan Police had limited resources to manage a crime spree of such severity. Detectives were under intense public pressure, as newspapers demanded swift action and citizens feared for their safety. Despite their efforts, the foggy streets, dark alleys, and the dense population made the work extremely difficult.

After Mary Ann Nichols was discovered on August 31, 1888, police officers arrived at Buck's Row to examine the scene. They took statements from witnesses and tried to identify anyone who had seen her shortly before her death. Early reports suggested she had been drinking with friends the night before, and she was known to frequent the Whitechapel area. Officers faced the difficulty of piecing together events in a district filled with transient residents, immigrants, and individuals living on the margins of society. Many witnesses were reluctant to speak due to fear of reprisal or distrust of the authorities.

Detectives soon realized that the murders were not random acts of violence. The brutality of the attacks, particularly the precise mutilations of the abdomen, suggested that the killer had some knowledge of anatomy. Scotland Yard detectives considered whether the perpetrator might be a medical professional or someone with experience handling knives. This theory shaped the investigation, as police began looking for men with medical training or who worked in butcheries, slaughterhouses, or hospitals. However, the evidence remained circumstantial, and no clear suspects emerged.

The murder of Annie Chapman on September 8, 1888, intensified the investigation. Chapman's body was discovered in the backyard of 29 Hanbury Street, and the crime scene was carefully examined. Detectives noted similarities to Nichols' murder, including the throat cuts and abdominal mutilations. This indicated a possible serial killer, a concept that was still new to law enforcement at the time. Police began coordinating efforts to track patterns, visiting lodging houses, interviewing local residents, and patrolling the streets more rigorously. Yet, the dense population and foggy conditions limited their ability to catch the perpetrator.

The investigation faced other obstacles as well. Forensic science in 1888 was rudimentary. There were no fingerprint databases, limited understanding of blood evidence, and no systematic collection of trace evidence. Detectives relied heavily on witness statements, suspect interrogations, and visible clues at crime scenes. This meant that mistakes were common, and promising leads often went cold. The Ripper's ability to blend into the streets and vanish after attacks made tracking him nearly impossible.

Elizabeth Stride and Catherine Eddowes, killed on the same night, September 30, 1888, presented new challenges for police. The "double event," as it came to be called, suggested a boldness in the killer and forced authorities to expand their search. Eddowes' murder included more extensive mutilations than Stride's, and forensic examination revealed details about the timing and possible movement of the killer between the two locations. Police officers increased foot patrols, attempted to block escape routes, and tried to identify suspicious men in the area, but the sheer volume of the population and the darkness of the streets worked against them.

The investigation also included collaboration between local police and detectives from Scotland Yard. Senior officers, including Chief Inspector Frederick Abberline, coordinated inquiries, but communication was slow and sometimes disorganized. Detectives attempted to cross-reference information from multiple murders, but the lack of centralized records made this cumbersome. The public, meanwhile, demanded answers, and newspapers published sensational stories, which often hampered police efforts by spreading misinformation or creating false leads.

The role of witnesses was critical but unreliable. Many people reported seeing suspicious individuals near the crime scenes, but identifying a suspect in a densely crowded district was extremely difficult. Residents' accounts often conflicted, and some were motivated by attention or personal grievances. Police officers had to sort through dozens of tips daily, but most proved to be dead ends. These challenges slowed the investigation and increased public frustration.

Letters sent to the police and newspapers during this period added another layer of complexity. Some claimed to be from the killer, boasting about the murders, while others were hoaxes. Officers had to evaluate the authenticity of these letters carefully, but they were often inconclusive. The letters added to the public's fear and fascination, making the investigation even more urgent in the eyes of society.

Throughout the investigation, social and economic conditions in Whitechapel affected the outcome. Poverty, overcrowding, and transient populations meant that many residents were constantly moving or hiding from authorities. Women who were at risk often lacked protection, and the community's distrust of police limited the flow of information. Detectives worked tirelessly, but the environment in which the crimes occurred was heavily stacked against them.

By the end of 1888, the investigation had revealed patterns and possible leads, but the identity of Jack the Ripper remained elusive. Police officers were exhausted from constant patrols, interviews, and analysis, and the public continued to demand results. The challenges of forensic limitations, social distrust, and the killer's cunning created a complex puzzle that would remain unsolved, leaving a legacy of fear and fascination that endures to this day.

Chapter 5: Letters from the Killer

During the height of the Jack the Ripper murders, a series of letters began arriving at police stations and newspaper offices. Some claimed to be from the killer, taunting authorities and describing the murders in gruesome detail. These letters added a new dimension to the case, creating both fear and fascination in the public, while presenting investigators with difficult questions about authenticity.

One of the earliest and most famous letters was received by the Central News Agency on September 27, 1888. Known as the "Dear Boss" letter, it was signed "Jack the Ripper," the first time the killer had used this name. The letter described the murders and threatened more violence if the police did not catch him. Although some police officers initially suspected it was a hoax, the letter gained attention when the name "Jack the Ripper" was printed in newspapers. The public and press quickly adopted the name, giving the unknown killer a lasting and terrifying identity.

The contents of these letters were often disturbing. Writers claimed knowledge of the crimes, including details about the victims' wounds and the killer's movements. Some letters were sent directly to Scotland Yard, while others went to newspapers, hoping to capture public attention. The writers of these letters sometimes used crude language and taunts, suggesting a dark sense of humor or a desire to manipulate public perception. The graphic nature of the letters heightened fear in Whitechapel and across London, contributing to the sensation surrounding the murders.

Among the letters, several stand out for their notoriety. The "Saucy Jacky" postcard, received shortly after the "Dear Boss" letter, described the murders in rhyming verse and included chilling references to the killer's activities. Another letter, known as the "From Hell" letter, arrived at George Lusk of the Whitechapel Vigilance Committee. It contained a small box with half of a human kidney, supposedly from one of the victims, and a note claiming that the writer had eaten the other half. This letter horrified the public and police alike, raising questions about whether the letters were genuine communications from the murderer or the work of hoaxers seeking attention.

Police faced major challenges in assessing the authenticity of these letters. Thousands of letters were received during the investigation, but most were quickly dismissed as hoaxes. Handwriting analysis and content evaluation were rudimentary at the time, making it difficult to determine which letters were credible. Detectives had to rely on small details, such as knowledge of crime scenes or medical terminology, to identify potential genuine correspondence. Even then, certainty was elusive, and many letters remained subjects of debate for decades.

The letters influenced both the investigation and public perception. Newspapers printed excerpts or full texts, increasing fear and fascination across London and beyond. The press played a significant role in shaping the image of the killer as intelligent, cruel, and elusive. Public interest soared, with many people reading daily updates and speculating about the identity of the mysterious Jack the Ripper. The letters turned the murders into a media sensation, demonstrating the power of print journalism in the late Victorian era.

The impact of the letters also extended to law enforcement strategy. Detectives debated whether the killer was literate, educated, or attempting to mislead authorities. Some believed the letters indicated a level of sophistication, while others thought they were the work of attention-seeking individuals unrelated to the murders. These debates influenced the focus of police inquiries, guiding searches for suspects with particular skills, occupations, or social backgrounds.

Even today, the letters remain a key element of the Ripper case. Scholars and crime historians continue to analyze them for clues about the killer's identity and psychology. Techniques such as handwriting comparison, linguistic analysis, and forensic testing of paper and ink have been applied to these historical documents, but definitive conclusions remain elusive. The letters contribute to the enduring mystery, as they may reflect the real killer, imaginative hoaxers, or a combination of both.

The letters also reflect the social environment of Whitechapel. Many residents lived in fear, and the letters intensified this anxiety. Women walking alone at night faced a heightened sense of danger, and families worried about vulnerable members. The letters demonstrated how communication, media, and rumor could shape public perception and amplify the psychological impact of crime. They became as much a part of the story as the murders themselves.

Finally, the letters illustrate the interplay between crime and media in Victorian London. Public fascination with the sensational, the gruesome, and the mysterious was growing, and newspapers competed to publish the most dramatic accounts. The Jack the Ripper letters offered a unique combination of horror and intrigue, allowing both the public and criminals to interact with the press. This relationship between crime, media, and public attention is a defining feature of the case and contributes to the legend of Jack the Ripper.

Chapter 6: Suspects Then and Now

The investigation into the Jack the Ripper murders produced numerous suspects, both during the late 19th century and in modern times. Over the years, theories about the killer's identity have ranged from plausible to highly speculative, and the mystery has fueled endless debate among criminologists, historians, and amateur sleuths. Examining both historical and contemporary suspects helps to understand the challenges faced by investigators and the enduring fascination with the case.

From the beginning, police focused on men living or working in Whitechapel who might have access to the victims and the skills necessary to commit such violent acts. Local residents, particularly those who had interacted with the victims, were questioned. Many suspects were dismissed quickly due to lack of evidence, but some remained under closer scrutiny. The investigative methods of the time relied heavily on witness statements, circumstantial evidence, and intuition, which made mistakes inevitable.

One of the most frequently mentioned historical suspects was Montague John Druitt, a barrister and teacher who disappeared shortly after the last canonical murder in 1888. Druitt's mental health had reportedly declined before his disappearance, and his death in the Thames River led some investigators to consider him a possible Ripper. Supporters of this theory argue that his timing, opportunity, and background could match the killer's profile, while critics note there is no direct evidence linking him to the crimes.

Another prominent suspect was Aaron Kosminski, a Polish immigrant and hairdresser living in Whitechapel. Kosminski suffered from mental illness and was confined to an asylum later in life. Some investigators at the time suspected him because of his proximity to the murders and his erratic behavior. Modern interest in Kosminski has intensified due to DNA testing on a shawl believed to have belonged to Catherine Eddowes, though the validity of these results remains disputed among experts. The lack of conclusive evidence means Kosminski's connection to the murders is still debated.

Michael Ostrog, a Russian-born criminal, was also considered a suspect. Ostrog had a history of violent behavior, theft, and imprisonment. Police believed he might have been responsible for some of the murders due to his criminal record, but contemporary investigators found no definitive links to the Whitechapel killings. His inclusion in suspect lists highlights how law enforcement often focused on individuals with criminal histories, even when circumstantial evidence was weak.

George Chapman, also known as Severin Klosowski, was a Polish-born barber and serial poisoner. Chapman was later convicted of murdering several women by poisoning in the early 1900s. Some historians have speculated that he might have been responsible for the Ripper murders, based on his presence in London at the time and his later violent crimes. However, differences in method—poison versus stabbing and mutilation—make this theory less convincing to many experts.

Contemporary investigations have introduced new suspects and revived old theories. Some researchers have suggested that high-profile figures, including doctors, aristocrats, or even royalty, could have been involved, though most of these claims are speculative and lack verifiable evidence. Modern forensic science has allowed for re-examination of letters, clothing, and other historical artifacts, but no definitive identification has been made. The challenge lies in the limited physical evidence and the degradation of materials over more than a century.

One modern approach has involved psychological profiling. Experts attempt to reconstruct the killer's personality based on crime scene behavior, victim selection, and the nature of the attacks. These profiles suggest a man with strong violent tendencies, likely familiar with anatomy, and capable of planning his crimes while blending into society. While profiling provides insight into potential characteristics, it cannot definitively identify a suspect, leaving conclusions open to interpretation.

Other historical figures occasionally suggested as suspects include James Maybrick, a Liverpool cotton merchant, and Francis Tumblety, an American quack doctor. Each has supporters and detractors among researchers. Maybrick's alleged diary contained confessions, though its authenticity is highly debated. Tumblety's presence in London at the time of the murders and his history of anti-women sentiments have made him a candidate, but again, evidence is circumstantial.

The diversity of suspects, ranging from local men to foreigners, professionals, and criminals, demonstrates the uncertainty and difficulty of the investigation. Police had to navigate misinformation, public hysteria, and limited technology, which allowed numerous theories to flourish. Even today, amateur detectives continue to explore archives, forensic evidence, and historical records, seeking a solution that remains elusive.

The focus on suspects then and now also highlights changes in criminal investigation techniques. In 1888, police relied on eyewitness testimony, handwriting analysis, and personal knowledge of the community. Today, investigators can use DNA analysis, advanced forensic methods, and digital reconstructions. Despite these advancements, the case remains unsolved, underscoring both the cunning of the killer and the limitations imposed by historical circumstances.

Ultimately, the study of suspects—historical and contemporary—reveals the enduring mystery surrounding Jack the Ripper. While some individuals appear more plausible than others, no single candidate has been universally accepted. This uncertainty continues to fascinate both scholars and the public, and it reinforces the perception of the Ripper as an enigma whose identity may never be conclusively determined.

Chapter 7: Modern Forensics and New Clues

Over a century after the Jack the Ripper murders, modern forensic science has given researchers new tools to examine old evidence. Techniques unavailable in 1888, such as DNA analysis, advanced fingerprint testing, and chemical analysis, have allowed experts to revisit the case with fresh perspectives. These modern methods aim to uncover information that was previously impossible to detect, offering the hope of new insights into one of history's most notorious serial killer mysteries.

One key source of evidence is the physical artifacts connected to the victims. Items like shawls, clothing, and letters have been preserved in archives or private collections. In some cases, forensic scientists have tested these objects for biological traces such as blood, hair, or tissue. For example, a shawl said to belong to Catherine Eddowes has been studied using DNA techniques. Some researchers claimed that mitochondrial DNA matched descendants of known suspects like Aaron Kosminski. However, critics argue that contamination, degradation over time, and uncertain provenance make these results inconclusive. Still, such studies illustrate how modern science can provide possibilities that 19th-century investigators could only imagine.

Handwriting and linguistic analysis of letters also benefit from modern technology. Specialists compare the writing style, phrasing, and vocabulary of letters purportedly from the killer to determine authenticity. While handwriting experts today can use computerized tools for analysis, conclusions remain uncertain. Many letters were likely hoaxes, complicating efforts to separate genuine communications from false ones. Linguistic analysis can suggest the writer's region, education, or social background, but it cannot definitively identify an individual.

Advances in crime scene reconstruction have allowed historians and investigators to better understand the conditions in which the murders occurred. Using maps, photographs, and survivor accounts, researchers can recreate the streets of Whitechapel, including alleyways, tenements, and public squares. Computer modeling and geographic profiling techniques help to identify likely routes the killer may have taken, escape points, and areas where the murders could have been committed unnoticed. This approach provides a clearer understanding of how the Ripper may have operated, even though it cannot confirm his identity.

Forensic pathology has also contributed to new insights. Modern pathologists can re-examine autopsy reports, looking at wounds, timing of attacks, and the sequence of mutilations. Analysis of these details can suggest the killer's handedness, possible use of instruments, and the level of anatomical knowledge. Some experts argue that the precision of the abdominal mutilations indicates a familiarity with human anatomy, possibly from medical training or butchery experience. Such conclusions help refine suspect profiles, even when definitive identification remains out of reach.

DNA technology, while promising, faces significant limitations in this case. Biological material from 1888 is often degraded, contaminated, or incomplete. Even where samples exist, establishing a direct link to a specific individual is extremely challenging. Researchers must account for over a century of handling, storage, and environmental exposure. Despite these obstacles, DNA analysis continues to be applied to hair, blood, and tissue remnants, with careful attention to scientific rigor. Each study adds potential clues, though none have yet produced a universally accepted result.

Digital archives and online databases have also transformed Ripper research. Investigators can now access historical newspapers, police records, and personal diaries with unprecedented ease. This allows for the cross-referencing of information that would have taken months or years in the past. Modern researchers can track movement patterns, social networks, and witness statements more efficiently, identifying new patterns or inconsistencies that may have been overlooked by original investigators.

Behavioral profiling, informed by modern criminology, provides another avenue for understanding the killer. Experts analyze patterns in victim selection, crime scene behavior, and escalation of violence to construct psychological profiles. Such profiles suggest a man motivated by control, rage, or psychological compulsion, who likely operated with careful planning and the ability to blend into society. While behavioral profiling does not identify a specific person, it narrows the range of potential suspects and helps historians understand the killer's mindset.

Some modern theories suggest that there may have been accomplices or that multiple individuals were responsible for some of the murders. Although most evidence supports a single killer, forensic reevaluation of timelines, geographic data, and witness statements allows researchers to reconsider these possibilities. While speculative, these alternative theories demonstrate the evolving nature of Ripper research and the role of modern tools in challenging long-held assumptions.

The application of new technology has also sparked public interest. Documentaries, books, and online discussions frequently highlight forensic breakthroughs, drawing attention to the enduring mystery. This interplay between science, media, and public curiosity mirrors the sensationalism of 1888, though now with the potential for empirical evidence rather than purely anecdotal speculation.

Modern forensics has not solved the Jack the Ripper case, but it has expanded our understanding of the murders, the environment in which they occurred, and the possible characteristics of the killer. From DNA testing to digital reconstruction, each new approach brings researchers closer to answering questions that have remained unanswered for over a century. The combination of historical records and scientific innovation continues to offer hope that the mysteries of Whitechapel may one day be illuminated more fully.

Chapter 8: Myths, Media, and Public Fascination

The Jack the Ripper murders captured the imagination of the public as much as they terrified it. Newspapers, pamphlets, and periodicals of the time sensationalized the crimes, fueling fear and fascination across London and beyond. The media played a central role in shaping the legend of the Ripper, turning a series of brutal murders into a story that continues to captivate people more than a century later.

Newspapers competed to provide the most dramatic accounts of the murders. Headlines emphasized the horror, describing mutilations in graphic detail and portraying the killer as a shadowy, intelligent predator. Sensational language and repeated coverage made the events impossible for the public to ignore. Readers followed each development eagerly, often forming opinions about the killer's identity and motives before police had completed investigations. This intense attention amplified the panic within Whitechapel and beyond, while creating a narrative of suspense and danger that was almost theatrical in its effect.

Pamphlets and penny dreadfuls, cheaply printed stories sold to the working class, also contributed to the spread of Ripper mythology. These publications often mixed fact and fiction, embellishing known details or imagining encounters between the killer and victims. While some stories were clearly fictionalized, they reinforced the idea of a clever and ruthless murderer stalking the streets. The line between reality and fiction blurred, with readers unsure which details were accurate and which were the product of imagination.

The letters allegedly sent by the killer added another layer to the public fascination. Newspapers published portions of the "Dear Boss" letter and the "From Hell" letter, giving the killer a voice in the media. Readers could see the threats and taunts directly, heightening the sense of personal danger and suspense. The letters contributed to the image of Jack the Ripper as a calculating, almost theatrical figure, controlling both his victims and the public perception of his crimes.

Public fascination was not limited to fear. Many people were intrigued by the mystery itself, trying to solve it through amateur detective work, correspondence, or social observation. Public meetings were held to discuss strategies for protection and investigation, and citizens were encouraged to report suspicious individuals. This sense of participation in the case reflected a broader cultural engagement with crime and justice in Victorian London, where the public eagerly consumed accounts of criminal activity and sought to understand it.

The media also played a role in shaping the identity of Jack the Ripper. By printing the name, emphasizing the brutality of the crimes, and reporting on the letters, journalists created a persona for the killer that transcended the real person behind the acts. This persona influenced both contemporary fears and modern interpretations, as authors, filmmakers, and historians continue to portray the Ripper in ways influenced by the original press coverage. The myth of the Ripper as a shadowy, intelligent, and elusive figure owes much to the way newspapers and pamphlets framed the story.

Photography, though less common than print, also contributed to the fascination. Crime scene photographs and images of Whitechapel provided visual context for readers, making the danger tangible. People could see the alleyways, streets, and buildings associated with the murders, reinforcing the immediacy of the threat. These photographs, combined with descriptive reporting, created a vivid mental image of the environment in which the murders took place, further capturing public imagination.

Over time, the story of Jack the Ripper grew beyond the specifics of the murders themselves. Authors, historians, and filmmakers have explored the case in novels, documentaries, and films, often emphasizing the mystery and horror. The Ripper has become a symbol of urban danger, social decay, and the dark side of human nature. Cultural representations frequently blend fact and fiction, continuing the tradition established by Victorian-era newspapers and penny publications.

Public fascination has also been fueled by speculation about the killer's identity. Hundreds of books, articles, and documentaries have proposed suspects, motives, and conspiracies. Readers and viewers are drawn to the puzzle, attempting to piece together clues from letters, police reports, and forensic evidence. This engagement demonstrates the enduring power of the case, as people are compelled by the combination of historical fact, human tragedy, and unsolved mystery.

The case also reflects social anxieties of the time. Fear of the unknown, suspicion of outsiders, and concern for women's safety in urban environments were all amplified by the murders and media coverage. The Ripper became a figure around which these anxieties coalesced, representing broader concerns about crime, poverty, and morality. The mythologizing of Jack the Ripper cannot be separated from the social context in which it emerged, as newspapers, pamphlets, and public imagination collectively created a legend that persists today.

Even today, public fascination with Jack the Ripper is evident in tours, books, films, and online communities. Whitechapel's streets continue to attract visitors seeking to understand the historical events, while scholars and enthusiasts debate theories, analyze evidence, and propose new interpretations. The media-driven legend established in 1888 remains central to the enduring interest, demonstrating the lasting influence of reporting and storytelling on collective memory and cultural perception.

Chapter 9: Theories and Controversies

The Jack the Ripper case has inspired countless theories and controversies over the years. Despite extensive investigations in 1888 and modern forensic efforts, no one has conclusively identified the killer. This enduring uncertainty has created fertile ground for speculation, conspiracy theories, and debates that range from plausible to highly imaginative. Understanding these theories helps to explain why the Ripper case continues to captivate historians, criminologists, and the public.

One of the most widely discussed theories is that the murders were committed by a single individual acting alone. This view is supported by patterns in victim selection, crime scene behavior, and methods of attack. The canonical five victims—Mary Ann Nichols, Annie Chapman, Elizabeth Stride, Catherine Eddowes, and Mary Jane Kelly—share similarities in age, occupation, and social vulnerability. Each was murdered in secluded areas, and the attacks displayed escalating brutality, suggesting a single person's evolving behavior rather than multiple unconnected perpetrators.

Other theories propose that more than one individual may have been involved. Some researchers argue that differences in timing, method, or location between the murders could indicate the presence of accomplices or copycat killers. The "double event" of September 30, 1888, when Stride and Eddowes were killed on the same night, has fueled speculation that the killer may have been interrupted, or that multiple attackers were active simultaneously. While the single-killer theory remains dominant, these alternative scenarios continue to spark debate.

A range of suspects has generated controversy over the years. Historical suspects such as Montague John Druitt, Aaron Kosminski, Michael Ostrog, and George Chapman have supporters and detractors. Druitt's mental health and disappearance, Kosminski's asylum confinement, Ostrog's criminal history, and Chapman's later crimes all provide circumstantial evidence. However, the lack of definitive proof means that none can be confirmed as the Ripper. Modern suspects, including James Maybrick and Francis Tumblety, often rely on disputed documents, such as diaries or anecdotal accounts, leaving their involvement highly controversial.

The authenticity of letters from the killer has also been a source of controversy. Thousands of letters were received by police and newspapers, but most were dismissed as hoaxes. Among these, the "Dear Boss" letter, the "Saucy Jacky" postcard, and the "From Hell" letter remain the most famous. Scholars and forensic experts debate whether any of these letters genuinely originated from the murderer. Analysis of handwriting, linguistic style, and content has produced conflicting conclusions, leaving the letters' credibility unresolved.

Modern forensic claims have added further debate. DNA analysis on a shawl allegedly linked to Catherine Eddowes has suggested a connection to Aaron Kosminski, but critics question contamination, degradation, and chain-of-custody issues. While such studies provide exciting possibilities, the limitations of century-old evidence prevent absolute conclusions. This ongoing discussion demonstrates the tension between hope for resolution and the practical challenges of historical investigation.

Theories involving high-profile individuals or conspiracies have also emerged. Some suggest that doctors, aristocrats, or even members of the royal family may have been involved or that there was an effort to cover up the crimes. While these claims are widely dismissed by scholars due to lack of credible evidence, they illustrate the human tendency to fill gaps in knowledge with speculation. Sensationalism continues to fuel interest in the case, blending historical fact with imaginative storytelling.

Psychological theories provide another layer of analysis. Behavioral profiling suggests the killer may have suffered from sexual dysfunction, aggression, or deep-seated psychological disturbances. Some experts argue that the killer demonstrated a mix of planning, opportunism, and familiarity with the urban environment. The precision of the abdominal mutilations points to some anatomical knowledge. These insights help shape understanding of the killer's mindset, even if they do not lead to identification.

The controversies surrounding Jack the Ripper also include the number of victims. While the canonical five are widely accepted, other murders in Whitechapel and surrounding areas have been considered potential Ripper crimes. Researchers debate whether additional victims share the same modus operandi or whether they were unrelated. This discussion reflects the broader difficulty of distinguishing between a serial killer's work and other violent crimes in a dense, impoverished urban environment.

Finally, the enduring controversies are part of what keeps the case alive. Disagreements among historians, criminologists, and enthusiasts ensure that new theories continue to emerge. The combination of limited evidence, historical distance, and public fascination allows multiple interpretations to coexist. Theories and controversies surrounding Jack the Ripper are therefore not just a reflection of the crimes themselves, but of society's ongoing desire to solve an unsolvable mystery.

Chapter 10: The Legacy of Jack the Ripper

The story of Jack the Ripper has left a lasting mark on history, criminology, and popular culture. Over 130 years after the Whitechapel murders, the name still evokes fear, fascination, and curiosity. The Ripper's legacy is complex, encompassing social, historical, and cultural dimensions that extend far beyond the East End of London.

One of the most significant aspects of the Ripper legacy is its impact on policing and criminal investigation. The murders highlighted the limitations of law enforcement in crowded urban environments and exposed weaknesses in evidence collection, forensic methods, and communication. Police techniques were rudimentary, relying heavily on witness statements, basic medical observations, and public tips. Today, the Ripper case is often studied in criminology courses as an example of how serial crimes challenge traditional policing methods and how investigative practices have evolved over time.

The case also influenced the development of forensic science. Modern techniques such as DNA analysis, crime scene reconstruction, and behavioral profiling have been applied retrospectively to the murders, providing insights that were impossible in 1888. The Ripper murders are sometimes referred to as the first well-known serial killings in modern history, and they inspired advancements in how law enforcement approaches violent crime. Researchers continue to analyze old evidence, testing theories about suspects, timelines, and methods, showing that even historical crimes can benefit from modern science.

Culturally, Jack the Ripper has become a symbol of the dark side of urban life. The case highlights the dangers faced by women in poverty-stricken neighborhoods, and it reflects broader social issues of the Victorian era, such as economic disparity, limited social support, and public fear of crime. Literature, film, television, and tourism have perpetuated the legend, turning Whitechapel into a site of historical and macabre interest. Walking tours, museums, and exhibitions explore the streets where the murders occurred, often emphasizing the atmosphere of fear and mystery.

The Ripper's story has also shaped the genre of true crime. Authors, journalists, and historians study the case not only for its historical significance but also for its lessons about human behavior, societal vulnerabilities, and media influence. The fascination with the unknown aspects of the case—the killer's identity, motives, and methods—has inspired countless works of fiction and nonfiction. True crime enthusiasts analyze evidence, revisit archival materials, and debate theories, contributing to a culture of investigation and storytelling that continues to grow.

The role of the media in shaping the Ripper legacy is particularly notable. Newspapers in 1888 created a persona for the killer that persists today, and the sensational reporting established a model for crime coverage. The letters purportedly sent by the killer, coupled with vivid reporting of the murders, created a sense of personal engagement with the public. This interplay between crime and media has influenced how society perceives high-profile cases, demonstrating the power of narrative in shaping collective memory and historical identity.

Another enduring element of the legacy is the public fascination with mystery and the unknown. Despite extensive research, the killer's identity remains unconfirmed. This unresolved aspect keeps the story alive, inviting new theories, forensic investigations, and historical debates. The uncertainty surrounding the case allows for ongoing engagement, as people are drawn to the challenge of solving a historical puzzle while grappling with the limits of available evidence.

Jack the Ripper's legacy is also intertwined with lessons about social vulnerability. The victims—Mary Ann Nichols, Annie Chapman, Elizabeth Stride, Catherine Eddowes, and others—were marginalized women living in poverty, often exposed to violence and neglect. Their stories highlight the dangers faced by disadvantaged populations and remind modern audiences of the importance of social protection and community support. The case underscores how social conditions can create environments in which crimes are more likely to occur, and how systemic issues influence individual vulnerability.

Educationally, the Ripper case serves as a tool for teaching history, criminology, sociology, and forensic science. Students and researchers study the murders to understand Victorian London, urban poverty, the development of modern policing, and the evolution of criminal investigation. The case offers an intersection of social history, human behavior, and scientific inquiry, making it a valuable resource across multiple disciplines.

Finally, the Ripper's legacy endures in the imagination of people worldwide. Jack the Ripper has become a figure in folklore, literature, and popular culture, symbolizing both the fear of unknown evil and the human desire to understand it. His story continues to inspire books, documentaries, films, and research, ensuring that Whitechapel and its dark history remain part of global consciousness. The combination of real-life horror, unresolved mystery, and social context guarantees that Jack the Ripper will continue to fascinate scholars, enthusiasts, and the general public for generations to come.

Printed in Dunstable, United Kingdom